You Are on Your Way to Becoming a Top-Notch Soccer Player If You Can . . .

- trap a waist-high ball with the inside of your foot

- send the ball to a teammate with a well-directed instep kick

- keep control of the ball with short dribbling in a crowded area

- as goalkeeper, punch a high ball over the crossbar to prevent a goal

These are some of the points for playing good soccer that are covered in this book. Sharpen your skills by learning these moves and many more. Find your own strategy for being a winner in soccer!

BE A WINNER IN
SOCCER

Charles Coombs

illustrated with photographs

AN ARCHWAY PAPERBACK
Published by POCKET BOOKS • NEW YORK

Permission for photographs is gratefully acknowledged: North American Soccer League, pages 7, 19, 73; Soccer Journal, page 40; Tampa Bay Rowdies, page 112; Thompson-Tully Company, pages vi, 10. All other photographs by the author.

An Archway Paperback published by
POCKET BOOKS, a Simon & Schuster division of
GULF & WESTERN CORPORATION
1230 Avenue of the Americas, New York, N.Y. 10020

Published by arrangement with William Morrow & Company, Inc.
Library of Congress Catalog Card Number: 76-39850

ISBN: 0-671-41104-7

First Pocket Books printing September, 1980

10 9 8 7 6 5 4 3 2

contents

foreword

Soccer might be called the most international of sports. Players dribble the ball in Zambia the same way they do in Afghanistan. A goal in Rio de Janeiro counts exactly as much as a goal in Bangkok, or Berlin, or Birmingham. A player caught tripping in Moscow suffers the same penalty as the one in Chicago.

Soccer, in fact, has become a common interest throughout the world. Following the example of other nationals, Americans are learning what amazing things can be done with an inflated checkered ball without the use of hands. A soccer player can juggle the soccer ball off his toes, knees, head, shoulders, heels, thighs—and never let it touch the ground. He is as adept as a juggler in a circus.

Americans are now flocking to the sport in unprecedented numbers. They are finding challenges in soccer above and beyond most other athletic activities. In no other sport are skill, endurance, and enthusiasm more needed or better rewarded.

1

Although I tackled this book with some trepidation—how much interest in soccer is there in the United States?—I soon realized there was no cause for concern. I found youth leagues, high-school conferences, college teams flourishing everywhere. Weekend amateur and semipro leagues were competing year-round on public playgrounds and school athletic fields. Professional teams were thriving everywhere. Soccer in the United States definitely has come of age.

To gather information, I traipsed around to a number of schools, playgrounds, and pro pitches. There I watched, talked to, and shot pictures of players of all ages and both sexes. My main research and picture taking, however, took place at Pierce College, Woodland Hills, where Coach/Player Rudy Dompe and his team demonstrated and explained the fine points of the game. Nowhere have I seen young athletes working harder, displaying more enthusiasm, or having more fun than the many soccer players with whom I was in contact.

To all who made writing this book a most exciting and pleasant task, my many thanks.

Charles "Chick" Coombs
Westlake Village, California
1977

chapter one

THE GLOBAL GAME

Soccer is a dynamic game of fast-paced action. It is a game based on a simple set of rules, the most important and frustrating of which is that a player is forbidden to touch the ball intentionally with his hands while it is in play. (The one exception is the goalkeeper.)

Soccer is a game that emphasizes cleverness, strategy, and skill rather than power. It is a game of almost continuous motion, calling for great energy and endurance from its players. There are few time-outs, and these pauses are short and usually due to accidents, injuries, or substitutions. So moments of rest are rare.

The soccer player must be able to adjust to constantly changing situations of play. Perhaps one of his teammates rushes an opponent and hooks the checkered sphere away from him with his foot. Suddenly the action changes direction. Now the player must dodge around his defender and break into the clear. With a deft swing of his foot, his teammate sends a pass skimming his way. He stops it on his instep and traps it. But as he prepares to drive a shot past the goalkeeper, an opposing defender rushes in from the side, jars him with a legal shoulder charge, and separates him from the ball. Before he can recover, another opponent gets to the ball and with a towering kick clears it toward the opposite end of the field. The player must quickly abandon his attack and race frantically back to help defend his own goal. Back and forth, back and forth.

Such is the challenge of soccer, the game played and watched by more people than any other game in the world. An estimated seventeen million people make up nearly two thirds of a million soccer teams located in more than 140 countries spread around the entire globe. Actually, only in the United States and Canada is the game called soccer. This name serves to distinguish it from the other game of football (played more with the hands than with the feet) that has developed in these two countries. Elsewhere in the world the game we call soccer is more accurately known as football. The name soccer is derived from what was once called Association Football, generally short-

Soccer is a rugged game.

ened to Assoc, which eventually turned into soccer.

Soccer is a game played as much with the mind as with the feet. The player must be as alert as he or she is agile. A player's size has little importance in soccer. A big person may lack the speed and endurance essential to run the four to six miles involved in a game. On the other hand, a very small person may find the hard physical contact too rough and rigorous. So, although there are both large and small players on a team, soccer is a game primarily suited to the average man, woman, boy, or girl.

The origins of soccer are unclear. However, a sporting event similar to modern soccer was played by the Chinese some 2500 years ago. It was called *tsuchu,* which roughly translates into "kick a leather ball with the foot."

In early Christian times Greeks and Romans played a kicking game using an inflated cow bladder for a ball. Roman fighting legions took the game with them as a means of relaxing between battles. Thus, it is believed the Romans introduced soccer to England as early as the third century A.D. The British refined the game somewhat and, in turn, made it popular throughout the British Empire. By the 1830s soccer had come to the United States, but it was given little attention there.

The game lacked organization, and all sorts of loosely knit leagues and associations sprang up. But unifying progress was made, and today both professional and amateur soccer in the United States is governed by the United States Soccer Federation (USSF). Many states have their own amateur soccer associations, yet they, too, come under the jurisdiction of the USSF. Most youth soccer competition, the fastest growing area of the sport in the United States, is regulated by the United States Youth Soccer Association, also an arm of the USSF. Today only a few youth leagues run their competitions without some type of centralized control.

Since soccer is a global sport, there is need for a central governing body. In 1904, the Federation Internationale de Football Association

Pelé has been the world's most famous soccer player for many years.

(FIFA, or feefa) was established to coordinate soccer activities internationally. Currently FIFA is headquartered in Zurich, Switzerland. It has approximately 140 member nations, including about every soccer-playing country in the world. FIFA's word is law in organized soccer.

7

Not only FIFA, but virtually all other sub-organizations and associations in existence—amateur and professional—abide by a set of rules that were established by the London Football Association more than a hundred years ago. They are known as the Seventeen Laws, and they were so well thought out that they are still in effect. There have been certain minor revisions to make the game more interesting and competitive, plus a few modifications for adapting the game to the capabilities of young boys and girls. However, the original Seventeen Laws form the foundation of the game today.

The laws begin by describing the field of play. Ideally, a soccer playing field, or pitch, should be 115 yards long by 75 yards wide. However, anything between 100 and 130 yards in length and 50 and 100 yards in width is acceptable. Often the standard soccer field is modified to fit available space, playing conditions, or the age and skills of the players. This rectangular field is bordered by a goal line at each end and sidelines, called touchlines, running lengthwise. A flag on a five-foot pole marks each corner of the playing field. A midfield line stretches between the touchlines and separates the field into equal halves. At its center is a spot with a circle having a ten-yard radius around it. At kickoffs all opposing players must be outside this circle.

8

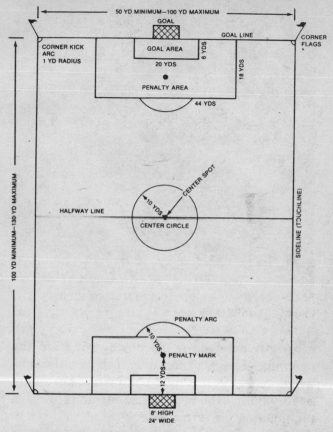

Soccer playing field, or pitch

Goals are located at the middle of each goal line. A goal consists of an open frame made of two side posts connected with a crossbar. The inside dimensions of the opening are eight feet high by twenty-four feet wide. Where possible a net should be stretched rearward and at about

Soccer balls vary slightly in size and weight for players of different ages.

a forty-five-degree angle downward from the opening. The net not only catches the ball when a goal is made, it eliminates any doubt as to whether the ball passed inside or outside the goalposts or crossbar.

A marked-off rectangle in front of each goal stretches six yards onto the field and is twenty yards wide. It is called the "goal area." Within this zone a player is not allowed to charge into or interfere with the goalkeeper when he or she has possession of the ball.

A much larger rectangular area surrounds the goal area. This so-called penalty area protrudes eighteen yards in from each goal line, and is forty-four yards wide. The goalie also is protected from being charged and interfered with within this larger area. However, the primary significance of the penalty area is that if a defending player commits a deliberate foul upon a goalward-bound player inside of it, the offended team is awarded a free penalty kick at the goal.

Finally, at each corner of the pitch a quarter circle having a one-yard radius is marked off inside the field of play. When a corner kick is taken, the ball is first placed on the ground within this arc.

Most soccer balls are constructed of black and white panels of leather or other satisfactory material sewn together to form the round sphere. The checkered design helps a player judge the type and amount of spin on the ball, which is a highly important aspect of the game.

The approved soccer ball must be no less than twenty-seven inches or more than twenty-eight inches in circumference. It should weigh between fourteen and sixteen ounces and be inflated to one atmosphere, which is equivalent to fifteen pounds per square inch (p.s.i.) at sea level. Actually, this description is for the professional Size 5 ball used by most teams. There is also a scaled-down Size 4 ball, which is used mostly by players under the age of thirteen.

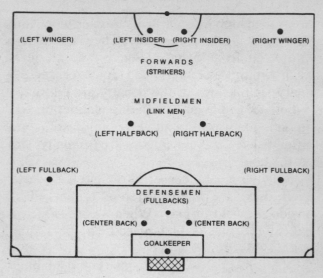

Basic positions in a 4-2-4 formation, which is just one of numerous player combinations

A soccer team is made up of eleven players, including a goalkeeper. Any player on the team may change places with the goalie during a lull in the game, provided he or she informs the referee and dons a different colored uniform (usually a simple slipover jersey) to maintain the distinction of the goalie from the other players on the field.

Soccer players dress simply and inexpensively in shorts, jerseys, calf-length protective socks, and blunt-cleated soccer shoes, traditionally known as boots, although today they are lightweight, low cut, and do not resemble

12

boots at all. Many amateur teams settle for tennis shoes, but cleated boots provide better footing and control of the ball.

Although shin guards are often worn under socks, there is no need for shoulder pads, hip pads, helmets, and other protective devices commonly used in football. Most amateur soccer players in organized competition need furnish only their own boots. The remaining uniform items usually are provided by a sponsor.

A soccer game is controlled by a referee. He enforces the rules, assesses penalties, keeps a record of the game, and even serves as the timekeeper. He is usually aided by one or two linesmen, although he makes the final decisions. In such an action-packed game, the referee's job is at times an overwhelming one. Much thought is now being given toward easing his burden by adding assistants as is done in baseball and football.

A standard soccer game is made up of two equal periods of forty-five minutes each, with a short half-time intermission. Youth games usually reduce the time to two thirty-minute halves.

The game starts with a team kicking off from the center spot and trying to move the ball toward the opponent's goal without use of the hands. The ball remains in continuous play until it crosses a touchline, until an actual goal has been made, or until the game has been stopped by the referee's whistle. Substitutions usually are made during these short pauses in the action.

A goal is scored when the whole ball has passed over the goal line between the goalposts and beneath the crossbar. It must get there without the use of hands, other than an accidental deflection off the hands of the defending goalkeeper or any of his teammates. Each goal counts one point, and the team scoring the greater number of goals wins the game.

To keep a game safe and under control there are, in addition to the seventeen laws of play, nine rules of discipline. Players must never kick an opponent. Nor are they allowed to trip him, jump on him, or charge him in a violent or dangerous manner. A charge from behind, perhaps the most hazardous kind, will surely draw a major foul. Furthermore, players must not strike or even attempt to strike an opponent. They cannot hold or push an opponent with their hands or arms. Lastly, they cannot catch, touch, hit, or in any way propel the ball with their hands.

Players will be penalized if they break any of these rules. The severity of the penalty depends largely upon whether the foul was accidental or intentional. The referee also takes into account where the foul took place and will usually assess a more severe penalty when it hinders someone's chance of scoring a goal. A player who fouls flagrantly or with excessive violence, or who uses abusive language, may be ejected from the game, and no substitute is allowed to take his place.

Basically, these rules of play are followed around the world. Soccer is a game in which each member of a team plays a full, strenuous, and exciting role. Often it is considered the supreme test of athletic ability.

chapter two
TRAINING OF A PLAYER

In order to play a good game of soccer, you must be able to "do it all." You must run, dodge, bend, kick, feint, and juggle the ball with your feet and head. You must be able to do everything but catch and throw. If you're a goalkeeper, you must also have those skills. In addition, you must have a keen sense of anticipation. You must know what is happening around you at all times and what is liable to happen next.

Furthermore, you must have an enormous amount of endurance. In no other sport is there the constant action found in soccer. The field is large, and the game almost never stops. There are practically no time-outs, usually few substitutions, and only brief periods of letup before you are back in the middle of the melee.

Using the foot to control the ball

So no other game makes more physical demands of its players than soccer. You must resolve to get fit and stay fit, if you want to play. Yet the rewards of playing one of the finest team sports in the world are well worth the effort.

Soccer stresses the use of the feet. The human animal has become more adept with hands than with feet, so soccer is not a natural sport. Dexterity with the feet requires a great deal of training and practice.

Soccer is primarily a running game. First and foremost in your training you must learn to run and keep running. Running itself is no great problem. You've been doing it most of your life. The more rapidly you put one foot in front of the other, and the longer stride you take, the faster you go. Still, running is a skill you can improve upon with practice. Do short wind sprints. Run hard for twenty yards, rest a few moments, then dash another twenty yards. Do these sprints again and again. Now run the length of the field at medium speed. Go back. Run a lap or two around the track. Also practice running with short strides, which give you better balance and ball control when dribbling. At all times work toward improving your running form. Keep your toes pointed straight ahead, raise your knees, lengthen your stride, and keep your arms pumping rhythmically in the opposite direction of your legs. In this manner you can develop the form and speed that will get you up and down the field in the shortest length of time.

But running in a soccer game is not like running in a track meet. Soccer is a mixture of jogging and dashing, running backwards and sideways, dodging and pivoting. So don't do too much straight running. Mix things up. You can set up an obstacle course of stakes, chairs, or whatever. Put them around in disarray, and work out several routes for dodging in and out around them. Jog, sprint, feint, and spin. Pretend someone is trying to catch you. You can do this exercise with or without a ball at your feet, although using a ball as you develop your

There is a continual scramble for the ball during play.

running techniques is a more rewarding way to practice.

Run with a teammate. Play follow the leader. Whether you simply try to outrace each other, or whether you go one-on-one in a running, dodging game of keep away, you will develop your running skills.

Although explosive speed has great value in soccer, agility counts even more. How good are you at changing direction? A soccer ball seldom travels a straight line for long. A foot deflects it, a head bounces it off in an opposite direction, a body stops its flight. Your job is to follow the ball, to be able to switch in midstride

19

from offense to defense, or vice versa. This instant change of momentum is easier for a light person than for a heavy one, and small feet are usually more agile than large feet. Hence, you should keep your weight in control.

Speed and agility depend primarily upon skill in using your feet and legs. But the rest of your body must be supple enough and strong enough to absorb the rigors of running and the jarring physical contact. You develop suppleness and flexibility for soccer just as you would for any other sport or physical activity. Do your knee bends and body twists as you warm up for a game. Touch your toes and swivel your hips. Do push-ups and sit-ups. Exercise the muscles of your arms, shoulders, neck, back, trunk, and legs. In this way you will be fairly relaxed and ready to play. You will avoid pulled muscles and lessen your chances of being injured during the game.

Muscular strength also comes primarily through exercise. Lifting barbells will help to strengthen arms, legs, trunk, and back. These muscle-building exercises are particularly beneficial when you are getting yourself in shape for the coming season. Stretching exercises, however, improve muscle tone more than weight lifting.

Try isometric exercises in which you pit muscular pressure against a resisting force.

Warm up well before a game.

Stand in a doorway with your arms down at your sides. Then push outward against the doorjambs with the outside of your hands. This exercise brings arm and shoulder muscles into play. Also, standing close to the doorjamb, push against it with your foot and leg. This exercise helps strengthen the muscles you'll use in side-to-side footwork.

Lie on your back and put a weight—say a box of books—on your stomach. Push it up and down with your abdominal muscles. Along with sit-ups, this exercise is an excellent way to strengthen your middle body.

There are endless techniques for strengthening muscles. You will benefit from almost anything that puts stretch and strain on them.

Sit-ups that include heading the ball to a teammate
are strenuous but excellent training.

Continue going beyond the first feelings of exhaustion. The more you do, the more you are able to delay fatigue during a game. The longer you can put off exhaustion, the greater your endurance becomes. Probably endurance, more than any other single quality, is a soccer player's most valuable asset.

Endurance is simply getting yourself and keeping yourself in such fine condition that you can hold your pace from the opening kickoff to the final whistle. Endurance is the sum total of all your efforts. Endurance results from keeping lungs, heart, muscles, and your whole mental attitude in the best of condition.

Eat properly, and keep your weight down. Go heavy on vegetable and protein foods, easy on fats and sweets. If you have any temptations concerning the use of tobacco, alcohol, or drugs, forget soccer. You'll never have what the game demands.

Exercise—and exercise some more. Know in your mind that you are a winner. Commit yourself to the game. Give it your best, physically and mentally. Dedication is what makes great soccer players.

chapter three
BALL CONTROL

The more time you spend with your soccer ball, the better you get to know it, the greater your chances will be of becoming a top-notch soccer player.

You must learn to control the ball. You must master it. You must be able to stop it, tame it, and move it skillfully against your opposition. Ball control involves such important skills as trapping the ball, kicking it, hitting it with your head, doing anything you can to get possession of it and move it without using your hands or arms.

In a soccer game the ball is constantly in motion, rolling or bouncing across the ground, or sailing through the air. Your primary job, regardless of whether you are on offense or defense, is to stop the flight of the ball, bring

Underfoot trap

it at least to partial rest at your feet, and take over the action. In soccer parlance, bringing the ball under control is known as catching and trapping. Often it is simply referred to as trapping. To trap a ball is to stop its flight with any part of your body or limbs other than your hands and arms. You kill its momentum so it will fall at your feet rather than bounce away where an opponent can get it.

The most common traps are made with the feet, for more often than not the ball is bounding across the ground. When the ball rolls toward you, time its pace and raise your foot just enough to wedge the ball beneath the sole of your shoe and the ground. Take care not to raise your foot too high, however, or the ball will go right on through. If you don't raise your foot high enough, the ball may bounce over or off it. The sole-of-the-foot trap is most effective for slow-rolling balls. Yet skilled soccer players can use sole traps on almost any kind of moving ball, including long, booming kicks that land at their feet.

Another common foot trap is done with the inside of the foot. As the ball approaches you, lift your foot a little off the ground and face the broad area between your big toe and heel directly in the path of the ball. Catch the ball against this slightly dished-in part of the foot, making contact as close to the center of the ball as possible. Let your foot give way upon

Inside-of-foot trap on a rolling ball

contact. The faster the pace of the ball, the more flexible your leg and foot must be in order to cushion the flight and allow the ball to drop softly to the ground.

As soon as the ball touches the ground, pin it down gently with either the sole or the inside of your foot, ready to make your next move with it. Actually, you should try to get the ball moving quickly in the direction you intend to go with it. Doing so saves time and decreases the opponent's chances of blocking your effort. At the moment you make the trap, turn your foot a little in the direction you intend to go. In this way the ball is moving toward whichever sector of the field you have in mind by the time you pivot or take your first stride.

You can use the inside-of-the-foot trap effectively to stop waist-high balls. Simply get your foot up where the ball is, cushion its flight, and let it drop at your feet. Often you need to lean back somewhat in order to get your leg and foot up high enough to reach the ball. Regardless of the location or pace of the ball, the inside-of-the-foot trap probably will prove to be your most effective means of getting possession of the ball. Practice it a lot, perhaps with a teammate, or bounce and retrieve the ball off some kind of a wall or backboard. If you don't have a soccer ball, practice with a tennis ball, bouncing it off a wall or garage door, trapping and controlling it. Practic-

Trap a ball any way you can, getting foot or body on
it to deaden its flight.

Instep trap

ing with a small ball makes controlling a larger ball much easier.

You can also trap the ball with the outside of your foot. This technique is particularly effective with balls coming in from the side. Often you are not in position or don't have time to turn the inside of your foot toward the ball. So, instead, you face the outside of your foot to the ball, cushioning it on the broad surface between your heel and little toe. Upon contact, let your foot give just enough to kill the pace so the ball drops to the ground. As the ball drops, wedge it momentarily under your foot, or nudge it gently in the direction you plan to go. The outside-of-the-foot trap is not as reliable as the inside-of-the-foot trap. But soccer is based largely on the ability to get one's foot or body in the way of the ball somehow, so do whatever works best at the moment.

Thus, when the ball is bouncing or falling toward you, you may naturally catch it on your instep, right on your shoelaces. This trap takes fine timing and a real feel for the ball. The boney instep of your foot is narrow and curved. Unless you catch the ball just right, it will bounce or ricochet off to the side. So you must let your foot go limp upon contact in order to maintain control. Keep your eyes on the ball, judge its pace and direction, and lift your foot off the ground in order to intercept its flight. In

Outside-of-foot trap

effect, when the ball makes contact with your instep, you simply lower it quickly and smoothly to the ground in one relaxing motion. Practice juggling a ball up and down off your foot in order to get the proper feel of the ball on your instep.

Although most of your traps will be made with your feet, you can also trap the ball with your thighs, stomach, chest, or head.

To execute the thigh catch, bring your knee up so that your upper leg is about parallel to the ground and facing into the path of the ball. Catch the falling ball on the upper surface of your thigh between your knee and hip. Your thigh is usually soft enough to cushion the ball, and you need merely to relax it a little upon contact to deaden the fall and let the ball drop in front of you. Once it is on the ground, you can trap the ball momentarily under your foot while you decide what to do with it next.

If the ball comes to you on a low trajectory, or maybe on a fast bounce, you can use a belly trap on it. To do so, put your stomach directly in the way of the ball. You bend inward a little upon contact and let the ball drop at your feet. Belly stops are not very common, but they come in handy at times when you must trap the ball any way you can.

For most high balls, a chest trap is more effective. Very often a kicked ball comes arching down out of the sky toward you. Keep your

Thigh catch

eyes on it. As it approaches, adjust your position in order to make a target of your chest. As the ball is about to make contact, lean back and push your chest up and out to meet it. Spread your arms wide for balance and to get them out of the way of the ball. As the ball hits, let your chest cave in around it. With its impact thus deadened, the ball will bounce only a few inches off your chest, just enough to clear it from your body and legs as it caroms down to your feet.

You can use the chest trap also to stop a hard, line-drive kick. You may even have to leap high in order to get your chest up into the ball's path. As the ball hits, let your chest sink back under the force. Hunch your shoulders in around it and lean forward in order to direct the ball to the ground, where you can trap it under your foot or start off in any direction with it.

Balls that you cannot reach with your chest can be trapped with your head. (This maneuver is not the same as heading, which has a different purpose.) In this trap you use your head to stop the ball and bring it under control. Perhaps the idea of putting your head in the way of a fast-flying, one-pound ball may seem reckless. It really isn't, not when done properly. Of course, you must be able to judge whether a ball is coming too hard to handle this way.

A high-bouncing ball or a ball looping toward

Chest trap

you at a safe speed can readily be trapped by keeping your eyes on its approach, adjusting yourself slightly to its trajectory, and meeting it with your forehead. Bend your knees to cushion the impact. Make the contact above your nose and eyes, at about the hairline, which is the toughest area of your skull. Keep your neck firm, but withdraw your head a little to deaden the jolt and allow the ball to drop within easy reach. A little practice at juggling a ball up and down off your forehead should give you the skill and confidence to perform head traps. They are simple and effective.

Head trap

As you may have noted, the primary purpose of trapping a soccer ball is to deaden its pace and deposit it at your feet so that you have effective possession. Indeed, this particular area of ball control is the foundation upon which the rest of the game is built.

chapter four
DRIBBLING, KICKING, HEADING

There are three primary ways to move a soccer ball. You can dribble the ball with your feet in order to control it until you find the right moment to get rid of it. You can kick the ball to pass it to a teammate, to clear it downfield and out of immediate danger, or to take a shot on goal. You can head the ball, that is, strike it with your head, in order to ricochet it toward a teammate or toward the goal.

Each method for moving the ball has specific techniques. You must master all of them in order to become a skillful soccer player.

When dribbling, you move the ball downfield with a series of gentle tappings of the feet, dodging around and trying to befuddle your opponents as you go. You must play the ball close to your feet, moving it this way and that,

Dribbling requires intricate footwork.

keeping it always within your own reach but beyond that of the opposition.

To dribble successfully, you need to use both feet. In fact, soccer is always a two-footed game. There is no way you can become a top-notch soccer player unless you are nearly as skilled with your weak-side foot as with your strong-side foot. Any opponent who discovers that you have a weak side will certainly take advantage of that weakness. So, if you are naturally right-footed, you must put in extra work and practice with your left foot until you are almost as adept with it as you are with your right.

Dribbling is a delicate skill requiring great deftness with your feet. Use the more sensitive forward part of your foot, up near the toes. Depending upon the direction you want to go and the speed you want to make, you alternate between nudging the ball with the forward inside of the foot and the forward outside. You may tap it one way with the inside area of your big toe, run with it, then change direction with an outside-of-the-foot tap when you see your opponent closing in on you. Of course, for further deception, which is what dribbling is all about, you must switch rapidly from one foot to the other, dodging and feinting all of the time.

There are two basic types of dribbles—short and long. Short, or close, dribbling is for use

When dribbling, use your body to shield the ball from your opponent.

in tight quarters where the main objective is to keep control of the ball until you can find a time and place to kick a pass to a teammate or take a shot on goal. Use both feet to move the ball one way and another as you try to deceive your opponent and keep him off balance.

Dribble long for speed. When you make a breakaway and are heading downfield with open space ahead and no one to kick the ball to, you may resort to the long dribble. Your taps become more like soft kicks, as you drive the ball well ahead of you, chase it, and dribble it again. Just don't let the ball get too far out ahead, where you risk losing it to an alert and quick-footed opponent.

When dribbling long, you should favor your strong foot for more positive control. Also, as you are moving speedily downfield, dribbling with the outside of your foot is faster and more natural. Turn your toes inward just before contact; and keep pushing the ball forward with each stride or two. However, if an opponent races up alongside, jockeying into position to get at the ball, switch your dribble to the far foot, thus putting yourself between him and the

Passing kick

ball. This screening of the ball is highly important if you are going to maintain control of it.

Dribbling at any time is risky, somewhat slow, and should be used only in situations where you are unable to kick a pass to a teammate. Generally speaking, a ball kicked at the goal is called a "shot." A kick to a teammate is called a "pass." The techniques are quite similar; only the purposes differ.

Usually kicking is a much better way to move the ball than dribbling. A good passing kick, which keeps the ball in your team's possession as you move toward your opponent's goal, is a major key to victory. Unpracticed or careless passing is a sure way to lose the ball.

The prime considerations for any kick are its accuracy and speed. Accuracy means to get the ball to a teammate's feet, so he can take it without breaking stride and continue goalward. To do so, you usually need to lead him a little, sending the ball to the open spot that he will reach in the next seconds. Through practice you will become familiar with his moves and be able to anticipate where he will be to receive your pass.

You put the speed, or pace, on the kick that is necessary to cover the distance between you and your receiver quickly and accurately. If he is nearby, you may nudge or tap the ball to him. If he is some distance away, you will need to kick your pass hard and low to him in order

Eyes down, swing your instep solidly into the ball.

to avoid an interception. Sometimes you can chip it high in order to loop the ball over the opposition.

The most important and most used kick in soccer is the instep kick. You approach the ball at a slight angle. Keeping your head down and your eyes on the ball, you plant your non-kicking foot beside it. Now you swing your kicking foot into it, turning your toes down and out enough to avoid stubbing them on the ground. This twist of the foot brings the broad surface of your instep—the area of the boot-laces—against the ball. The more instep surface you get on the ball, the better the power and accuracy. This kick is the one that has been adopted so widely for kickoffs and attempted field goals in the American game of football. A booming kick, it is good for maximum velocity and distance. You can adjust the height and distance by raising or lowering your point of contact on the ball and gauging the force of your swinging foot. The instep kick is essential to good soccer. It is a major weapon on both offense and defense. Practice it diligently.

A less widely used but no less important kick in soccer is the inside-of-the-foot kick. It is one that affords maximum control and is used largely for short, accurate passes and fairly close-in shots on goal. As when making the instep kick, you approach the ball at a slight

Use the inside-of-the-foot kick for accuracy and short passes.

angle, with your head down and your eyes on it. With knees slightly bent, you plant your nonkicking foot beside the ball, as you swing your other foot forward. As your foot swings in an arc toward the ball, turn your toes upward and outward. Lock your ankle and bring the broad surface of your foot between your heel and the big toe against the middle of the ball. Follow through by continuing to swing your leg toward the target.

As is true of any kick, you determine the trajectory of the ball by choosing your point of contact. Usually you hit it at about dead center in order to keep it close to the ground. If you want to loft it high, put a little extra bend in your nonkicking knee, lower yourself, lean back, and kick the ball below its center, chipping it upward. As you become increasingly skilled, you will be able to kick the ball to the left or right of center to curve a pass around an opponent or bend a shot toward the goal corner.

A good soccer player seldom kicks with his toes, for the area of contact is small and accuracy is poor. Occasionally, however, a defenseman will use a toe kick to boom the ball far downfield and out of immediate trouble around the penalty area. But never use a toe kick when you can get into position for an instep kick.

One of the less common kicks is the outside-of-the-foot kick. Not effective for much distance or force, this kick is used more for short passes and to add deception to dribbling. To make it, you approach a rolling ball, keeping your eyes on it. As you reach it, turn your toes downward and lock your ankle inward so contact with the ball is made just behind the toes on the outer edge of the instep. You nudge or jab the ball to move it ahead or to the side as you wish. The outside-of-the-foot kick is often used to punch the ball sideways to a teammate running alongside you.

Other types of kicks are good for specific situations. Nearly half of the balls that come your way during a game will be on the fly. On a large percentage of them you will not have the time or opportunity to trap the ball and bring it under control while you decide what to do with it next. Therefore, you must field it on the fly. You must get a foot onto it and kick it immediately in the direction most beneficial to your team. This kicking the ball in flight is called volleying.

Until you get the hang of it, a well-controlled volley kick is difficult to make. Positioning and judgment are all-important. For your most accurate volley kicks, use the broad inside of your foot. Get your foot up to the ball in much the same manner that you would for an inside-of-the-foot trap. However, instead of deadening the ball by letting your foot sag back upon

A volley kick on a descending ball

50

impact, you kick right on through the ball, aiming it as best you can. The inside-of-the-foot volley is most effective on balls coming at you about knee height or slightly lower.

Although you can sometimes get the inside of your foot up and onto a ball that is higher than your knees, you will usually be better able to volley it off your instep. To get your instep up and into its path, you probably will have to lean back somewhat, spread your arms wide for balance, and swing your leg up almost horizontally. Again, you should make contact on the slightly dished surface of your instep.

The high volley is not easy to handle with accuracy. But your main concern is to get a foot up and on the ball to deflect it. However, with practice you will learn to control the high volley.

On a low volley, down near your feet, point your toes down, lean a bit over the ball, and swing your instep straight into it. Depending upon the tilt of your foot and the position of your body over the ball, you can volley kick it low or high.

Volley kicks are good anyplace on the field. Use them when there is scant time to trap and control the ball. Use them to clear the ball far downfield and out of danger. Also, a volley kick is effective deep in your opponent's territory for a quick, forceful shot on goal.

Sometimes when you are unable to reach the

ball on the fly, you must kick it just after it hits the ground. This play is not unlike a no-hands dropkick and is known as a half volley. When properly timed so that you get the instep of your foot onto the ball just as it rises from the ground, you can turn it into one of the strongest shots of a game.

A couple of other less used but dramatic kicks are the overhead volley and the backheeling kick. You use the overhead volley when you are facing in the direction away from your opponent's goal and the ball comes flying toward you about chest height. Although you are facing the wrong way, you must make an effort to relay the ball on toward the goal. As it comes within range, you lean far back and kick your foot up at it. You cock your toes upward to make a right angle with your ankle. In order to get your kicking foot up high and onto the ball, you need to bring your nonkicking foot up off the ground also. To do so, you make a scissoring motion with your legs. Thus, with both feet off the ground and airborne, you bring the instep of your angled foot into the ball as you kick it rearward over your head.

When executing this kick, you find yourself lying on your back in midair, so you must project your hands downward to help break the fall. Then pick yourself up immediately and get back into the game. The overhead volley has an important place in soccer, but it takes some

Overhead volley

practice and willingness to risk an occasional bruise.

Back heeling, which is used for dribbling as well as for kicking, is a bit of deceptive ball handling. While racing downfield with the ball, you may find a defender suddenly blocking your path. Having noted that one of your teammates is following close behind you, you step over the ball and, with your heel, kick it quickly backward to your trailing teammate. The back-heeling kick is a short kick, but it often works effectively to prevent a sudden scramble for the ball.

Most of soccer is based upon the kicking of moving balls. Regardless of the distance or speed, whether it is a pass or a shot on goal, kicking is the essence of the game. To play good soccer, you most devote a major amount of your attention to kicking.

To back heel, step over the ball and pass it rearward.

But, important as it is, kicking is not the only way to move a soccer ball. At certain times and in certain situations, you must be able to move the ball with other parts of your body, excepting your hands and arms. You may pass a ball by ricocheting it off your chest. You may carom it off your knee or hip or turn your back to it and bounce it off your shoulders. But a more accurate and much more common way of directing a bouncing or flying ball toward your teammate is with your head. Indeed, a head shot on goal has scored many a winning point. Heading is essential to the game of soccer, and players use their head to move the ball frequently and effectively.

There is a definite technique to proper heading. First of all, you must keep your eyes steadily on the ball as it comes toward you. If you take your eyes off it, you are apt to misjudge its trajectory and get hit on the top of the head or, even more painfully, on the nose.

As you watch the ball come toward you, adjust the level of your head so that contact will be made on the forehead, at about the hairline. Above all, don't wait for the ball to hit you. Go to it. Attack it. Use your neck muscles as shock absorbers. Keep your eyes open until the last moment, at which time you are bound to blink. Just before contact is made, thrust your forehead into the ball. You can thrust up under it to send it high, or you can leap up and bring your forehead down to angle it toward the ground. With a little practice, you can use a flick of your neck at the time of contact to send the ball in any direction you desire. Whether passing to a teammate or leaping up and deflecting the ball into the goal, "kicking with your head" is a fundamental of winning soccer.

Soccer demands ball control. And ball control includes trapping, dribbling, kicking, and heading. By increasing your skill at each function, you become a winning player.

chapter five
CHOOSING A POSITION

One of the important decisions you must make when trying out for a soccer team is which position to play. Don't rush it. Take your time while making up your mind, and give each position on the team a tryout. Before long you and your coach will know which position you are best suited to play. In any case, there is not a great deal of difference in the play of the positions. In modern soccer every player relies upon the common skills of trapping, dribbling, kicking, heading, and, particularly, running. And everyone except the goalkeeper has the opportunity to score goals.

On the other hand, each position on the team calls upon certain special talents that should be considered when making a choice. A strong aggressive tackler usually makes a better defenseman than a forward; a deft dribbler and a sure-footed kicker make a better forward than a defenseman.

Nevertheless, to be a worthy soccer player these days, you must be able to switch roles with any teammate when necessary. Excepting the goalkeeper, each player on any team must be capable of roaming the field as long as a teammate is around to cover whatever position he or she may leave open.

The ten players of a soccer team in addition to the goalkeeper fit into three main kinds of positions on the field. They are the defensemen, the midfielders, and the forwards.

Defensemen patrol the high-danger area just in front of and to the sides of the goal. Usually they are called fullbacks. There are sometimes three but more often four of them, depending upon what formation a team uses. Of the four, the interior two are often called center backs, or perhaps left center and right center, while the outside two are usually the left or right fullbacks. All four form the final line of defense, in front of the goalie, against an attack by opposing forwards.

Defensemen are usually the huskier and stronger members of a team. To be a good defenseman, you need to be a good tackler, who can get a foot to the ball and steal it away from an opponent. You need to be a good header, who can deflect booming kicks and high passes away from the goal mouth. The taller you are, the more easily you can leap and get your head on the ball. There are also many occasions when you are unable to stop and trap a ball, so you must be able to volley kick it on the fly and out of danger.

As a defenseman you must be sufficiently fleet of foot to stay between your mark (the person you are guarding) and the goal. In doing so, you also try to crowd your opponent toward one of the touchlines, keeping him wide of the goal. Run alongside him. Jockey him and harass him so that he will have to get rid of the ball or won't be able to receive it. Since you are defending with your back to the goal, you must be able to run backward almost as well as forward.

Defensemen go two on one to steal the ball from an attacker.

Above all, as a fullback you must protect your goalie. This responsibility is especially important for the center backs who patrol the area directly in front of the goal and are usually in the middle of an attack. The outside backs are charged with protecting the flanks.

As a defenseman you ordinarily will not go beyond midfield when your team has the ball. But there are exceptions at selected times. In today's wide-open style of soccer playing, fullbacks sometimes go all the way downfield to help in an attack on the enemy goal. However, provision must have been made for a teammate to stay back and cover for you in case of a sudden turnover of the ball. This strategy is called overlapping and is an important tactic in modern soccer.

Most team offensive thrusts begin with the fullbacks. You may intercept a pass, make an out-of-bounds play from the sideline, or get a free kick. So you must be adept at all phases of the game. In short, a good defenseman is a good all-around player.

Stationed ahead of the defensemen are the midfielders. Usually there are two. As a midfielder, your function is to form a link between the defense and the offense. Thus, midfielders often are called linkmen. They are also called halfbacks, since they play halfway between the fullbacks and the forwards. Midfielders are the playmakers, who size up the field situation and

A fullback clears the ball upfield with a booming instep kick.

instigate an attack. They are considered the sparkplugs of the soccer machine.

To be a midfielder, you need to be quick, fit, and aggressive. You must be quick, because once you gain possession of the ball you must control it and relay it immediately to one of your teammates, usually a forward, before your opponents are able to set up an effective defense. Although you should be a good, tricky dribbler, the fastest and most effective way to move the ball is by kicking a pass. In either case you must be surefooted.

A linkman needs to be among the fittest on the team. In that position you are constantly on the move, running back to help your defense, running forward to aid the offense. Running, running, running. Many times you penetrate all the way to the enemy goal area and often take your own shots on goal. Thus, you are constantly trading positions with the forwards during the heat of an attack.

When not helping out your offense, you must hound the opponents, either trying to get the ball away from them or keeping them so off-balance that they cannot move the ball successfully. Your success in gaining possession of the ball and getting it quickly to one of your forwards will be a major factor in scoring.

Soccer being such a teamwork sport, no team without balanced strength can hope to win many games. However, there is no denying that forwards must be among the best players on the squad. Normally there are four forwards in a team's formation. Out on the flanks are the outside left and outside right, known generally as wingmen, or wingers. Then there are the inside, or center, forwards, sometimes called inside left and inside right, but more commonly known as strikers.

Thus, in a commonly used 4-2-4 balanced formation, a team (not counting the goalkeeper) has four fullbacks, two linkmen, and four forwards. But formations can be shuffled around in any manner that seems best suited to the occasion. If your team puts emphasis on

A striker moves in on a well-guarded goal.

defense, the player combination may be switched to 4-3-3 or even 4-4-2. (Soccer formations always start at the back and work forward.) In these cases, there are four defensemen and three or four midfielders. This strategy robs power from the forward line and requires midfielders that can switch roles and move into striker positions when launching an attack.

On the other hand, a team that is offensively minded may use a 3-2-5 formation. Although it steals a man from the defensive line, it adds a fifth forward to the attack. Such scrambling of formations puts added value on the soccer player who is sufficiently versatile to play any position on the team.

Although tall players have an advantage as they are able to leap up above others and head a flying ball into the goal, being tall is not at all essential for a forward. More important, in that position you must be fast, tricky, and an expert ball handler. Your main aim is to score goals, but getting into position to do so requires a sharp eye, quick feet, and the ability to feint and fool your adversary. Usually you work in close quarters around the goal, where everyone is dueling for the ball. You must be a deft dribbler and a sure kicker. An error during either maneuver is likely to turn the ball over to the opponents.

These days the outside forwards, or wingers, usually score as many goals as the inside forwards. Wingers are also largely responsible for passing the ball from the flank positions toward the goal mouth, where the center strikers attempt to deflect or head the ball into the cage. Such cross passes are not easy to make, and so a winger should play the side of the field that gives him the best chance to use his strong foot. If you are a left-footed winger, play the left side of the field; if you are right-footed, play the right side. Even though you must be adept at using both feet, you probably will not be able to use both equally well.

As a winger you need to be tricky enough and sufficiently fleet of foot to prevent defensemen from bottling you up in a corner or forcing you toward the touchlines. You should be one of the team's better kickers, able to drive a kick across the field or chip the ball over a

A forward needs power and control for kicking long shots on goal.

defender's head to a teammate. You must be agile at moving without the ball, pivoting and dodging and mixing up your defender as you maneuver toward the goal.

Most of the time, however, you play out on the edges of the pitch in order to keep the play spread out and reduce the congestion around the goal. The less congestion there, the better chance your inside strikers have of scoring.

As a winger you sometimes make out-of-bounds plays. You also may take the corner kicks after the ball, last touched by your opponents, goes out-of-bounds over the goal line.

In general, you control the ball along the touchlines, feeding it to your teammates in the goal area as quickly and accurately as possible. At any turnover of the ball, you immediately switch to defense.

If you prefer to be an inside striker, you will find yourself spearheading most of the goalward thrusts. To be an effective inside forward, you must be a totally versatile player. Although you may be charged primarily with scoring goals, you must be in the middle of the action at all times, regardless of where you are on the field or which side has the ball.

On offense, you must be a good leader and playmaker and an unselfish passer. You must be capable of dropping back quickly on defense to help cover opposing halfbacks in order that your own midfielders can lend aid to the hard-pressed fullback.

As a striker you must be adept at heading the ball into a goal. Many a crucial goal is scored by a striker leaping high above the congestion and heading a looping pass or a corner kick into the cage. You also must have extra skill as a kicker. There will be relatively few times during action around the goal mouth when you have time to line up a kick carefully. Often you have to play the ball on the fly. You have to be a cool kicker, ignore the clashing confusion around you, and somehow shoot the ball goalward.

As a striker you need to be rugged, for all of the goalward thrusts you make will be in, around, and through a crowd of determined defenders. You will be closely marked, for you are the main threat of any attack. You will be bumped, buffeted, and bruised. Unless you are able to feint, dodge, trap, and dribble, you will have little opportunity to get a shot on goal.

Half the time you play with your back to the goal as you maneuver around looking for a kick that you can bring under control or try to head into the goal. All the while the defense is breathing down your neck and ganging up on you. You need to stay calm and keep your mind on the game if you should get some blind-side punishment from others equally bent upon getting to the ball.

Probably another part of your job as a striker, since you should be one of your team's best kickers, is to take penalty kicks following an intentional foul made within the penalty area.

So each position on a soccer team calls for certain specialized skills. Some shoot better than others, some pass better than others, some tackle better than others. However, remember that, above all else, a good soccer player is a complete soccer player, proficient in all phases of the game.

chapter six
KEEPER OF THE CAGE

Being a goalkeeper is perhaps the biggest, undoubtedly the loneliest, and often the most critical job on the soccer pitch. As goalkeeper you are the final line of defense. Behind you is the unguarded cage, eight feet by twenty-four feet in size. As keeper of the cage, you have the difficult, bruising mission of preventing any of the opposing ten players from somehow forcing that checkered ball past you into the net.

On other parts of the field players usually pair up in one-on-one confrontations, a defender marking an attacker. In your case you don't enjoy any such single match up. Everyone is out to get you. So a player needs unusual talents, determination, and confidence to handle the pressure of goalkeeping. On the other hand, the excitement and the satisfaction are

A goalkeeper's nightmare is having the ball zip past his prone body and into the net.

so rewarding that few keepers care to trade positions with anyone else on the field.

Before you decide to become a goalkeeper, you should try the other positions on the team. Get an overall knowledge of the game, and learn the fundamentals of trapping, dribbling, kicking, heading, and tackling. You should know all the moves you will be called upon to make regardless of where you play on the field. Above all, you must learn to stay alert to all of the action around you and be able to anticipate what is likely to happen next. Once you are well acquainted with the game, you certainly should take a turn at goalkeeping, whether or not you intend to make it your regular duty.

In order to be an effective goalie, you should be somewhat on the large size. Being tall enables you to get up above the opposing players in order to catch or deflect the ball. Being solidly built helps prevent injuries and withstand the close-quartered banging and buffeting that takes place around the goal area.

But, above all, you need fast reflexes and sure hands. The hands are important, for, as goalkeeper, you are the one person on the team who is allowed to use them. Anywhere within the penalty area you are the one person on the team permitted to catch the ball, deflect it, throw it, or roll it with your hands. Of course, you also use your feet in much the same manner as the other players. But the use of your hands is the one advantage you have over the rest of the team.

The biggest use you will make of your hands is catching the ball. Although there are various other ways of preventing the ball from going into the net, the most common is to catch it, to get it in your hands for a moment. When you have possession of the ball within the penalty area, your opponents must leave you alone and give you a fair chance to get rid of it. You are allowed to take four steps before you kick it upfield or pass it off to one of your team-mates.

As a goalkeeper you will be bombarded with balls coming at you from different directions at all speeds—high, low, or to the side. Frequently the ball comes bounding across the ground toward you. When trying to catch it, you must first get your body in front of it to prevent it from slipping through your hands. If it is a slow roller, you may have time to go out to meet it. If it is a high-speed grass cutter, you must concentrate on getting down on a knee and stopping it with both hands and body. But avoid getting down on a knee when you are sure you can bend at the waist, scoop the shot up in your downturned hands, and lift it quickly to the protection of your chest. When you are down on a knee, you are at a disadvantage if the ball bounds away or if someone manages to deflect it out of reach.

Always beware if you are deep in the goal mouth. If, while catching the ball, you are jostled backward or inadvertently carry the ball back over the goal line, a score is counted for your opponents.

When catching high balls, you reverse the action of your hands. You watch the flight of the ball closely, judge its trajectory, then leap up and extend your arms fully over your head. Turn the palms toward the ball with your thumbs almost touching each other. Since you do not have the advantage of your body to back up your catch, you must prevent the ball from glancing off the palms of your hands or going right on through. So keep your hands slightly relaxed, reach out with your fingers, and as you wrap your fingers around the ball let it settle securely against your palms.

A well-executed leaping catch gets you up above the other players, who may be trying to jump and head the ball into the goal. Once the

Gather in a low ball and bring it quickly up against your chest.

A goalie makes a leaping save.

high catch is made, bring the ball down to the protection of your body until you decide what to do with it next.

Some of your most difficult and dramatic moments take place when you have to make a diving save. The checkered ball comes spinning out of a sea of churning legs. It heads for a corner of the cage. Not having had time to anticipate the shot, and unable to get your body in front of the ball, you face a desperate situation. Like a shortstop spearing his glove out to snag a scorching line drive, you launch yourself horizontally toward one of the goalposts, reaching far out with both hands for the ball.

Since you are lying flat out in the air, you take the ball in your fingertips and bring it quickly into the protection of your body while still falling toward the ground. With the ball secure, you now concentrate on breaking the fall by distributing the impact on an arm, shoulder, or hip. Just be sure to hang onto the ball.

Sometimes you will not be able to get your hands on the ball to catch a high or wide shot on goal. In that case, you must resort to whatever action you can come up with to keep the ball from going into the cage. One way is to leap and punch it off to the side or up and over the crossbar. Watch the ball and, as it arrives, drive one or, if possible, both of your fists toward it. Your doubled fists make an effective

The goalie must be prepared to make diving saves.

ram, but keep your doubled-up thumbs outside your fingers to prevent injury. Be sure to get enough fist on the ball to punch it out of danger.

When you cannot get your fists in position to punch the ball clear of the goal, you must deflect it in any way you can with foot or hand. A foot deflection is an unsure maneuver and should be used only in a most desperate situation when you cannot get your hands on the ball.

The safer and more common deflection is with the hand. With an open palm, or sometimes just your fingertips, you push the ball wide of the goal or up and over the crossbar.

When unable to catch a high ball, punch it up and over the crossbar with your fists.

You should be facing the ball, and the timing of your leap must be right. The primary purpose is to keep the ball away from the goal, so you must do what you can, any way you can. You don't have time to think about style or form.

Never try to punch or deflect a ball if you can catch it. Punching or slapping is a far less reliable way to control it. Also, after you have ricocheted the ball over the goal mouth or across the end line, your opponents retain pos-

The goalie should go out to meet the ball whenever practical.

session of it for a corner kick. Thus, although the deflection may have gained you a little time, you remain on defense within the dangerous area of your own goal.

Your basic defensive position should be directly in front of and a couple yards out from the goal mouth. But you must adjust this position constantly, moving to one side or another when the ball is being played along the touchlines. No matter where the action is taking place, even down at the far end of the field, you should keep your eyes on the ball. You must stay alert to all movements of players and the ball in order to anticipate and be ready to aid or counter the action. When the ball is far downfield, you should leave the goal mouth and move out near the edge of the penalty area. There you are closer to the play, and you are also away from the noise and diversions that so often take place around the ends and edges of the field.

The closer you are toward the action, the better you can act out your role as commander of your area. From your vantage point you can yell instructions to the players. "Hey, Joe, watch out behind you!" "Quick, Karen, cross the ball to Sue!" Communicate with your teammates. If a kick comes your way and several players converge upon it, shout "Mine," or "Goalie's," or whatever will make them peel off and leave it for you to catch. If you

The goalkeeper must constantly follow the movement of the ball.

decide to move out from the goal after a ball, shout to your fullbacks to cover the empty cage for you. Talking up the game helps.

When goalkeeping, you cannot simply wait back in the goal mouth and hope to stop well-placed shots. If an opponent races your way, dribbling the ball unmolested, you must rush out toward him. The closer you get to him, the less goal area he will have to shoot at. This strategy is known as narrowing the angle and is the same move that an ice-hockey goalie uses. Also, by moving out to meet a charge, you force the attacker to shoot more quickly and from farther out than he probably would like to.

The goalie is the last line of defense.

Just remember that when you move out, you must yell for your teammates to fill the gap behind you and protect the goal mouth. If not, the attacker may try to chip a shot over your head. If there is no one back of you to knock the ball down, the shot is an easy goal.

Although as goalie you are your team's last line of defense, you also are its first line of attack. Once you are in possession of the ball, you are the one who initiates a new offensive thrust toward the far end of the field. In other words, you must distribute the ball. You need to do so quickly, for you should get your attack started before your opponents have time to fall back and organize a defense. You normally distribute the ball by kicking it, rolling it, or throwing it to a teammate. In this way you retain possession.

However, at times you will want to clear the ball far downfield and out of immediate danger. So you punt it or dropkick it. Or you take a goal kick by placing it on the ground inside the penalty area and booting it as far downfield as you can. Such kicks, however, put the ball up for grabs by either team. So, when possible, you should pass to a teammate and retain possession.

Make your passes out to the side, away from the front of the goal, in order to avoid a possible interception. Choose whichever passing method is right for the moment. You can use an inside-of-the-foot kick for a fairly long pass. If your teammate is in the clear about fifteen or twenty yards away, your best and surest method for getting the ball to him is to roll it. Bend low and underarm it as you would a bowling ball.

For middistance passes you can use a regular overhand baseball throw. But don't loop it casually. Put some mustard on it so the opposition cannot intercept it. Baseball overhand throws of the fairly large soccer ball are not always easy for young players to make. You may prefer to use the stiff-arm throw, starting down near your knee and using your arm like a catapult.

Indeed, there are many things to learn in the process of becoming an effective goalkeeper. But after you have thwarted a few attacks, stopped a few shots on goal, and saved a few games, you will have earned the right to be the most satisfied player on the team.

chapter seven
THE OFFENSE

The mission of a soccer team with possession of the ball is to move it downfield as quickly and skillfully as possible and power it into the opponent's goal. Usually the best way to do so is the simplest and most direct way, based on the fundamentals that you have carefully learned and practiced. Victory depends largely upon the team's putting together the basics of trapping, dribbling, kicking, heading, and running.

Various methods are used to achieve this team effort. Soccer is not a heavily structured sport with a lot of set plays and restrictions on what you can do or where you can go. Of course, there are rules to keep the action within bounds, preserve safety, and make competitive sense out of what otherwise would become chaos on the field. But soccer players still enjoy a greater amount of freedom than is present in most other team sports. In soccer you go where you can do the most good and do whatever will aid the scoring of a goal.

Typical of this freedom is the use of overlaps. There is nothing in the rules telling you to stay back near the center line if you are a midfielder. A defenseman doesn't really need to remain around the far end of the pitch all the time. Inside forwards and wingers are not always the first ones down the field with the ball. When conditions are right, a midfielder, or even a fullback, can shift into high gear and go all the way down the field helping out the strikers on an attack or even getting out ahead of them. The maneuver sometimes befuddles the opposition, who may be marking the front-

The offense moves the ball goalward.

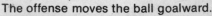

line players so closely that they give scant attention to defensive players. A sudden overlap of assignments upsets the defense's plans and quite often scores a goal.

Overlaps cannot be done in a helter-skelter manner, however. They must be planned, understood, and worked out in practice. Provision must be made for some other member of the team to cover for the aggressive back, or a sudden turnover of the ball will convert the surprise offensive thrust into a critical defense problem.

Although members of your team may enjoy considerable freedom of movement, you line up and operate generally within a fixed formation. You may adopt the basic 4-2-4, or you may prefer a more defense-oriented 4-3-3. If you wish to emphasize a strong offensive effort, you may choose a 2-3-5 formation. Whichever you use, most of the time you play your general zone and contend with your particular opponent. But there are no fences to keep you within your zone, and you try to go with the play regardless of your regular position—as long as someone covers for you. Soccer is a game of opportunities that quickly vanish unless you are prepared to take advantage of them.

One of your biggest jobs on offense is to shake loose from the player marking you. To do so, you try to find and occupy as much open space as you can. You must keep on the move, decoying your opponent, dodging and feinting and anticipating where a pass will come. This function of creating open space is one of an offensive player's major tasks. Getting out into the clear is about your only way of controlling the ball and getting a decent shot on goal.

So you must play as hard when you don't have the ball as when you do. After all, with twenty players on the field (not counting the two goalkeepers) the average amount of time you will possess the ball figures to be a mere 5 percent. Sometimes you will handle it much more than that, sometimes less. But, taking the average, 95 percent of the time one of your

You must keep playing whether or not you have the ball.

teammates or one of your opponents will have the ball. During those times, the way you play is just as important as when you have the ball.

You must size up the field situation as it unfolds. Perhaps you can decoy an opposing midfielder or defenseman out toward the touchline, so other members of your team will have a clearer path goalward. Or you may create some open space where you can take a pass. Run, jog, and run some more. Keep busy. You cannot help your team's efforts by waiting for the defense to send the ball back downfield. An attack cannot form if you kick the ball upfield and wait to see what will happen. Even though you may not be in the vicinity of the play at all times, be alert to what is happening and keep planning and doing anything you can to help get that ball and move it goalward.

Keeping the ball moving is the key to any offense. You can move it with a booming kick to clear it away from the penalty area. For power and distance, use an instep kick. For accuracy, use an inside-of-the-foot kick, aiming the pass to a cleared area where one of your teammates will have a chance to get to it first.

You can also move the ball by dribbling. This method is dangerous when you are down around your own goal, trying to get an attack started. A good tackle on the ball by an opponent can result in a quick score for the other team. At the far end of the field, however, in the close quarters around your opponent's goal, a bit of tricky dribbling and a snappy pass can set up a play with your wingers or center forwards, who can move in for the score. Your assist shares in the credit for the goal, and most goals depend upon a skillful assist.

Although dribbling has its place, the surest, quickest, and best way to move a soccer ball is with a series of well-executed passes. Try to keep the ball moving on the ground. Beware of cross passes in front of your own goal. An interception there gives a shot on goal to your opponents. So try to keep the ball moving upfield and preferably out near the touchlines, when you are on your own half of the pitch. Interceptions are not usually as costly when the ball is out near the fringe of the field. A few short passes to teammates who have "made a little open space" to receive it will get the ball upfield in a hurry.

Often a long clearing pass can set up a breakaway for the far goal. A breakaway is an exciting part of soccer, like a football player catching a pass and streaking sixty yards for a touchdown. As long as you are not offside at the beginning of the breakaway, you are free to surge on ahead and confront the goalkeeper in a one-on-one match up.

The offside rule in soccer states that there must be at least two players—a minimum of

A free kick clears the ball from the dangerous penalty area.

the goalkeeper and one other—between you and the goal, whenever the ball is passed forward to you on the opponent's half of the field. The reason for this rule (and it has changed from time to time) is to prevent a player on offense from simply hanging around the opponent's goal mouth and banging in a long kick that may arrive in the vicinity. Such a one-on-one situation would make the goalie relatively helpless.

There are certain situations when the offside rule is not in effect, and confusion sometimes results. To avoid problems, you should study the offside rule directly from the official laws of the game and get your coach's interpretation.

Since soccer is a foot-oriented game, there is lots of kicking to do on offense. There are, of course, the normal clearing kicks, passing kicks, volley kicks, and such. In addition, free kicks follow fouls, and a corner kick is awarded when the ball goes out-of-bounds over the goal line (wide of the goal itself) after last being touched by some member of the defending team.

If you are deliberately tripped, pushed, held, or charged at violently, the referee blows his whistle and you are awarded a direct free kick from the spot of the infraction. The ball is placed on the ground, and opposing players must keep ten yards away until you have played the ball. You may try to power a direct free kick straight at the goal, or you may pass it off to a teammate. When you are near the edge of the penalty area, you may be tempted to take a straight shot on the goal. Yet, to defend against a free kick (that is not a penalty kick) the opponents are allowed to form a shoulder-to-shoulder barricade between you and the goal mouth. So usually the better strategy is to pass the ball to a teammate and hope to launch a successful attack from the side. On any free kick you need only to nudge the ball so it rolls the length of its circumference to put it officially in play.

The Offense

When a foul is of minor nature and unintentional, the referee will award an indirect free kick in which the ball must be touched and played by at least one teammate before a goal attempt can be made legally.

By far the most serious of free kicks, a penalty kick, is awarded to you if a defender fouls you within the defensive penalty area. The punishment is severe, but it is deserved since fouls committed within the small area in front of the goal usually occur to save an almost sure score.

A costly penalty kick pits a team's best kicker against the goalkeeper.

On a penalty kick the ball is placed down on the penalty mark located twelve yards out in front of the goal. All other players, except the opposing goalkeeper, must clear the area. The goalie has the almost futile task of trying to protect the eight- by twenty-four-foot goal. Indeed, many games are won and lost through penalty kicks.

The threat of free kicks—indirect, direct, or penalty—goes a long way toward keeping control of a game. Soccer is not a sport in which you can get away with bad conduct, poor sportsmanship, and excessive roughness. It is a rugged-enough game without any of these violations, and anyone who stoops to them damages the team effort.

Another common kick that you will often take on the offense is the corner kick. You are awarded a corner kick from the corner flag nearest the spot where a ball goes out-of-bounds over your opponent's goal line, provided your opponent touched it last. (If your team touched it last, their keeper takes a goal kick to clear the ball out of danger of the penalty area.)

On the corner kick you set the ball down within the one-yard corner arc. Since opposing players must back at least ten yards, you can kick a short pass to a teammate or kick it wherever you wish, just as long as someone else touches the ball before you do so a second time. Players of top teams try to curve a booming inside-of-the-foot kick directly to the goal mouth, where teammates are waiting to leap up and head a high ball into the cage or volley kick a lower ball netward. Skilled corner kickers sometimes manage to curve the ball directly into the goal, an amazing offensive feat.

When a ball goes out-of-bounds over a sideline, having been touched last by an opposing player, you are awarded a throw-in instead of a corner kick. A throw-in is the one time during a game when you can use your hands on the ball. Of course, you are outside the playing field when you do so.

A throw-in, like a free kick or a corner kick, is called a restart, meaning that after an interruption in the action, your team starts the ball back into play. Throw-ins are very important, and most often are made by strong-armed midfielders, although anyone on the team can make the throw.

A throw-in must be made with the ball held in both hands and from directly behind your head. No sideways, underhand, or one-handed throw-ins are allowed. While throwing the ball you must keep both feet on the ground. One method is to stand with both feet planted just outside the touchline, arch your back, and whip the ball with both hands from behind your head. Sometimes you simply toss the ball toward the feet or head of a nearby teammate,

A legal overhead throw-in from the touchline

or if you are strong enough, you can heave the sphere all the way into the penalty area. Long, accurate throw-ins often catch the opposition unprepared and set up a shot on goal.

Another method is to place one foot behind the other while making your throw-in, thrusting off with your back foot, but keeping it scraping the ground until the ball has left your hands.

You can even make a running approach to a throw-in to add momentum and distance to the throw. Again, be sure that both feet remain on the ground, that you hold the ball in both hands, and that you do not step over the touchline and onto the field until the throw is made. There are no offsides during throw-ins or corner kicks, so you may feed the ball in any direction.

Practice throw-ins, for they are an effective means of getting an attack under way.

The final function of the offense is goal shooting. Regardless of your normal position on the team, in today's wide-open style of soccer, you undoubtedly will get your opportunities to take shots on goal. Rely on practiced fundamentals, trying first to establish control over the ball before kicking for a score. You needn't necessarily trap the ball and bring it to a stop first. The churning action around the goal mouth seldom allows such leisurely planning. But the ball should be squarely at your feet before you take your shot.

Powering a shot on goal

Your most powerful shots are made off your instep, with your toes pointed down and your ankle locked. Perhaps your most accurate close-in shots, however, can be made off the larger curved surface of the inside of your foot. You choose whichever style has the better chance of working under a particular set of playing conditions.

When time is short and confusion is rampant, and the ball sails down toward you out of the sky, you must swing a foot up and into the ball, volleying it on the fly, aiming it as best you can for an open corner of the goal. Normally try to keep your shots low and to a corner. A goalkeeper has a harder time trying to get down to block a low shot than to leap up and catch or punch a high one.

You need not always try to power your shot past the goalie. He is sometimes better prepared for a hard shot than for a sudden fake and a soft shot slipped slyly past him. Judge the situation and decide in midstride which type of shot has the best chance to score.

In addition, remember to make the best of any opportunity you have to leap up and head a high ball into the goal.

The variety of offensive moves you can make is endless. With patience and practice, your offensive game will come together and your team will enjoy the results.

chapter eight
THE DEFENSE

You will be of little value to a soccer team unless you become as adept at playing defense as you are at offense.

Your main mission on defense is to stop your opponent's attack and get possession of the ball. To do so, you protect an area or mark (guard) a man closely to cut off any threat upon your goal.

At times, when the action is well out in the middle of the field, and a tight defense is not necessary, you guard a zone rather than a particular man. Down near your goal you need to stick closely to your man, so he is unable to receive or handle the ball. You badger him and harass him and, should he get possession of the ball, try to separate him from it.

Usually a good defense combines both, zone

Defensemen turn back attacks on goal.

and man-to-man coverage. In any case, the
best way to keep your opponent from scoring
is to stay between him and the goal. Keep as
close to him as necessary to hinder his ball
handling. Yet you must be careful not to mark
him so closely that he might feint you out of
position, dribble or kick around you, and break
loose for a score. Above all, study your opponent's playing habits, so you will know how
tightly or loosely you should guard him.

Often you will switch from zone to man-to-
man and, on many occasions, go two-on-one
as you gang up on one of their star strikers,
who is working in dangerously close to your
goal. The midfielders must do the best they can
to prevent the attackers from filtering through.

When they fail to do so, the fullbacks must protect the goal. Actually, despite playing basic positions, all backs must be able to switch duties quickly in order to befuddle an attack and leave no dangerous gaps in the defense.

Once you have established your proper defensive position between your mark and your goal, try first to jockey him away from the action. Maneuver him toward the touchline, where he has little room to receive a pass. Even if he gets the ball, he is in an awkward position there to make a pass and has a poor angle at the goal. Forcing him out wide also cuts down on the number of players in front of the goal and gives the other defenders a better chance to single out their marks and stop an attack.

Although you should concentrate on the ball itself, you also must stay alert to everything else going on around you. This ability is sometimes called having a "field eye" and is an essential part of the game. With your field eye, you recognize an offense forming and know how to try and block it. Don't be afraid to call for help, if you see your zone suddenly being flooded with opposing players.

Usually, when you have your man under control, your next concern is to see that he doesn't get the ball. If he does get the ball, then you try to take it away from him. First of all, when the attacking team moves the ball downfield, get close enough to your man to attempt an interception if the ball comes his way. But don't cling too closely to him, for he may fake you one way, swing around you, take the pass, and have a clear shot on goal. Only experience and your estimate of the speed and deftness of your opponent can determine how closely you can mark him.

Interceptions are risky, but they are the backbone of a defense, and you must not hesitate to try and make them. When you intercept in the vicinity of your own penalty area, the action is usually furious. Accordingly, you should clear the ball out of the danger area as quickly as possible. You have little time to trap

Defensive positioning against a corner kick

it and set it up for a pass, and an attempt to dribble it is hazardous. So kick it upfield in any solid manner you can. If you have time, of course, aim it toward one of your forward players. Otherwise, boom it for distance. At the worst, if your opponents get to it first, they will have to re-form and try to launch another attack on goal.

Tackling is another good way to wrest the ball from a player. Although you are not allowed to tackle the player, you may tackle the ball in an attempt to dislodge it from your opponent. Since you are not permitted to use your hands, you tackle with your feet. A tackle in soccer is thrusting a foot out at the ball,

Legal tackle or a trip?

either drawing it away from your opponent's feet and toward your own or, as is much more common, knocking it away with your foot and hoping one of your teammates will get to it.

If you are going for the ball and not the player, the referee will not call a foul even if there is some body contact. A legal tackle is part of the game, which is why some players wear shin guards.

One tackle, called a block tackle, is made from the front. You confront your ball-handling rival and block his path. Get to him quickly, keeping your feet fairly close together so he can't suddenly dribble or kick the ball between your legs. Planting yourself solidly, lean toward him and bring the instep or the inside of your foot up against the middle of the ball. Chances are that your opponent will try to change direction with the ball and will become a little off-balanced. Since you have reached your foot in and are forcing the ball in the opposite direction, you should come away with it. Stay on your feet, and move away once you have possession.

The sliding tackle differs from the front or block tackle in that it is usually from the side and you must get down low, often right on the ground, to make it. A sliding tackle usually is made for the express purpose of knocking the ball away from an attacker. You seldom try to

A block tackle

gain possession of it yourself, but knock it
loose for a teammate to pick up.

You come in low from the side, plant the
foot nearest your opponent solidly on the
ground, lower yourself, and thrust the other
foot out at the ball. (You are not allowed to
jump at or try to kick the ball away with both
feet.) Be sure you get at least a toe on the ball.
If you miss the ball and trip your opponent,
you will be called for a foul. If you kick the
ball, however, and your opponent trips over
your foot, no foul is called. Frequently referees
must draw a fine line between what is a foul
and what is a legal tackle.

As you slide in low, reaching a foot out for the ball, you should lower your hands in order to break your fall. If you can, curl your non-reaching foot under you, like a baseball player making a hook slide into second base, and you will be able to spring up quickly and get back into the play.

There are variations and combinations of block and sliding tackles. Each is based on the main fundamental of going for the ball, not the man. Body contact is an unintentional by-product. Good tackling takes a bit of courage, a decent amount of strength, aggressive determination, and fine timing. But you must learn to do it, for the outcome of many a game hinges on a few missed or made tackles.

A sliding tackle

A permissible shoulder charge

The Defense

There is one form of intentional body contact in soccer that is permitted and plays an important part in any successful defense. It is called "shoulder charging," which is an accurate description. A shoulder charge, unlike a tackle, is used to get the player away from the ball, not the ball away from the player. A shoulder charge usually occurs when two players are racing beside each other in a duel for control of the ball. Then you can legally barge your shoulder and upper arm into your opponent's shoulder and upper arm as you attempt to get the ball.

But you cannot hit at him or flail out with your arm. You must keep it in close to your side. You shove your shoulder into your rival's shoulder with the intent of forcing him from the path of the ball, not of knocking him sprawling across the ground. If the referee decides your action is overly violent, he will call a foul on you. Also, the shoulder charge must be made from the side, not from behind your opponent.

Most defensive efforts made for the purpose of getting the ball rather than hindering the man are allowed. Of course, you cannot use hands. You play the ball as best you can within the few rules that are laid out, and the referee's judgment is final.

This freedom of action helps to make soccer the popular, wide-open game that it is.

chapter nine
SOCCER TODAY

Soccer in the United States has come a long way during recent years. No longer is it a foreign game. Of course, you are not likely to find any high-ranking team from the high-school level on up that does not include South Americans, Europeans, Australians, Africans, or Asians. Indeed, players come from all over the world. Yet many are Americans, and American young people now are taking to soccer. Youth soccer leagues are burgeoning in the United States. Young boys and girls from the age of five become familiar with the game and play it.

Most players delight in the freedom of modern soccer and the opportunity to get a turn at both offense and defense. Even the goalkeeper, whose duties are quite specific, usually trades off with other members of a team during the course of a game. Then he, too, can get into the running, dribbling, kicking, and heading fun of the contest.

Television brings soccer into the nation's living rooms. Commentators explain the game fundamentals to their unseen audiences. Any sports enthusiast who is willing to give the game a little attention soon discovers how exciting it is. Parents are exposed to their children's enthusiasm for and knowledge of the game. In many families, parents, sons, and daughters compete in soccer at different age levels and in different leagues.

A sign of soccer's increasing popularity in the United States is how much high-school and college teams have improved during the past decade. Many of these players are coming out of the neighborhood youth soccer leagues. Another encouraging development is that girls' soccer leagues are flourishing throughout the country.

Although professional soccer in the United States had an indifferent response in the beginning, it is now receiving widespread attention. There is good reason to expect that within a decade soccer will become one of the country's biggest sports and that the United States will soon field some of the best teams in the world.

Indoor soccer is yet another reason for the game's increasing popularity. Both amateur and professional soccer have moved onto boarded-over ice-hockey rinks, into school gymnasiums, and some auditoriums. Both the American Soccer League (ASL) and the North American Soccer League (NASL) sponsor indoor professional games. Where playing facilities are available, indoor school leagues have been formed.

Basically, indoor soccer is a scaled-down version of the game with similarities to ice hockey. The typical indoor team has six players—five players and a goalkeeper. Often their playing surface is a synthetic turf over ice. Due

Young players are a sign of soccer's increasing popularity.

Soccer is a team sport widely played by girls.

to the limited space, the defenders must be almost as good attackers as the strikers.

Teams play three twenty-minute periods.
There are usually no time-outs, except when
play is stopped after a foul or in case of injury.
Unlimited substitution is allowed while action
is under way. The soccer ball, like a hockey
puck, is ricocheted off the boards and kept in
play. Such continuing action in close quarters
stresses tight ball control, many shots on goal,
and a tight defense.

Indoor soccer is a high-speed, scaled-down version
of the game.

Long-clearing kicks cannot be used in indoor soccer, for the ball would go up into the stands. A game-delaying deliberate kick out-of-bounds sends the kicker to the penalty box for two minutes—a minor foul similar to that assessed in ice hockey. Another modification is that the goalkeeper has a small cage to guard. It varies anywhere from four to seven feet high by twelve to sixteen feet wide, depending upon the league and the size of facilities.

Indoor soccer is a great training ground for the outdoor game. Since it can be played any time of year, it enables a player to keep physically fit and maintain his sharpness of skills even when there is snow on the ground.

So soccer can be a good game for you even if you never intend to go beyond play in a youth league. On the other hand, you may someday become a member of the United States Olympic team. Or you may even reach the pinnacle of soccer competition and find yourself traveling to some distant land to compete in the World Cup.

No matter at what level it is played, soccer is a game of skill, strength, and endurance. It is always a pleasure and a challenge. What more could you ask for in a sport?

glossary

Back—a defender.

Breakaway—a dribbler gets clear of the defense and heads goalward.

Center—to kick the ball from the sideline area toward goal area. *See* Cross.

Center circle—circle with ten-yard radius in the center of the field, from which kickoffs are made.

Chip—to kick low on the ball sending it high in the air.

Cross—*see* Center.

Defender—a back primarily responsible for protecting the goal.

Direct free kick—a dead-ball kick that can be shot directly at the goal.

Dribble—use the feet to manipulate the ball.

Feint—to take an opponent out of position.

FIFA (feefa)—Federation Internationale de Football Association, the governing body of world soccer, headquartered in Zurich, Switzerland.

Foul—any act contrary to the laws of the game.

Forward—a front-line, attacking player.

Free kick—*see* Direct and Indirect free kick.

Goal—a rectangle eight feet high and twenty-four feet wide, bordered by corner posts and crossbar.

Goal area—an area six yards deep and twenty yards wide in front of goal.

Goalkeeper—keeper or goalie, the one player on the team who can use hands. The last player on defense.

Goal kick—an indirect kick taken to clear the ball away from the penalty area.

Goal line—boundary, or end line, marking the end of the field.

Halfback—a linkman, or midfielder, who plays between the fullbacks and the forwards.

Half volley—to kick the ball just as it bounces.

Heading—moving the ball by means of the forehead.

Heeling (back heeling)—playing the ball backward off the heel.

Indirect free kick—a dead-ball kick that must be touched or played by another player before a goal can be scored.

Instep—the top of the foot along the shoelaces.

Juggle—to keep the ball in the air with various parts of the body except hands.

Kickoff—a forward kick that starts each period of the game and puts the ball in play after each goal. Ball must travel the distance of its circumference before it is in play.

Linkman—*see* Halfback.

Mark—the opponent being marked, or guarded.

Marking—close man-to-man guarding of an opponent.

Midfielder—*see* Halfback.

Offside—a penalty that usually occurs when a player is nearer an opponent's goal than the ball at the time the ball is played to him and there are less than two opponents between him and the goal.

Overlap—a back joins the attack by running down the touchline past a forward.

Penalty area—a rectangular area eighteen yards deep and forty-four yards wide in front of the goal. Outside the smaller goal area.

Pitch—another name for soccer field.

Save—to prevent a goal.

Screen—protect the ball by keeping between it and an opponent.

Shoulder charge—a legal form of body contact in which two players shoulder each other out of the way to get at the ball.

Striker—an inside forward.

Tackle—trying to get ball away from an opponent by use of the feet.

Throw-in—restart the game by an overhead throw of the ball from outside the touchline after the ball has gone out-of-bounds.

Touchline—sideline.

Trap—to stop and get control of the ball.

Volley—to kick the ball while it is in the air.

Wing or Winger—forward who plays out wide near the touchline.

World Cup—the official international soccer championship held every four years.

index

indicates illustration

ABOUT THE AUTHOR

CHARLES COOMBS graduated from the University of California at Los Angeles. An athlete at school and college, Mr. Coombs began his career by writing sports fiction. He soon broadened his interests, writing adventure and mystery stories and nonfiction articles. He enjoys writing for young people and has published over a thousand stories and articles and many books, fiction and nonfiction. Mr. Coombs is married and has two sons and a daughter.